PRAISE

"RUN, REACH, RESPECT gives you the motivation to overcome the inertia in your life and create positive change by being proactive, setting and measuring goals, and valuing the impact of others."

Elaine A. Melonides
Global Leader & Consultant,
Real Estate Strategy,
Portfolio Optimization and Transformation

"We spend an inordinate amount of time working on strategy, operations, and tactics in our professional lives. Why shouldn't the same be true for our personal lives? RUN, REACH, RESPECT brings the insights of corporate leadership to personal development. The process cultivates a better, more intentional version of yourself."

Curtis Bailey
Founder, Quiet Wealth
Author, Quality Time Left

"Lists Lists Lists. I enjoyed all the checklists, graphs, charts, and bullet-list summaries proposed. The book is extremely interactive and kept me thinking a lot throughout the read. Several points stayed with me:
    'Time is our most precious resource, and it's the resource we all share equally.'
    'Expert advice is often the most undervalued or least considered means of expanding your circle.'
    'Improve Your Environment will also improve THE environment.'
All simple but true."

Calvin August
CPD Recruit, 114th Academy

RUN, REACH, RESPECT

THE GUIDE

THE GUIDE

RUN, REACH, RESPECT

Start each day with promise. End each day with progress.

LYDIA JACOBS-HORTON

JAKE ADVISORS, LLC
Cincinnati, Ohio

Copyright © 2023 by Lydia Jacobs-Horton

All rights reserved.

Cover design and interior page layouts by Sheila Hart Design.
Edited by Jennifer M. Evans and Alexandra Horton.
Published in the United States by JAKE ADVISORS, LLC, Cincinnati, Ohio.

www.runreachrespect.com

ISBN: 979-8-218-19367-6

Printed in the United States of America.

DEDICATION

To my parents,
Fred Michael Jacobs, Sr.
and
Elaine Salim Jacobs

You taught us a lot about a lot.

11
START EACH DAY WITH PROMISE

23
RUN

Get Active
24

Hydrate
28

Eat Nutrient-Rich
31

Restore
34

39
REACH

Practice Your Intention
41

Manage Your Money
46

Expand Your Circle
52

Read
55

59
RESPECT

Be Kind
60

Express Thanks
63

Improve Your Environment
65

Reflect
68

73
END EACH DAY WITH PROGRESS

CONTENTS

74
INTENTION PLANNER

78
FRAMEWORK

102
REFERENCES

START EACH DAY WITH PROMISE

Businesses grow and thrive by defining simple principles that drive progress. Principles inspire people to get started and to keep going in the direction that matters most. Personal progress can be inspired in the same way. Personal development books are helpful, but most are lengthy and not suited for quick application and early, sustained results. RUN, REACH, RESPECT changes this through specific rationale, sets of Actions, and a Framework that apply the most common business strategies to personal success. RUN, REACH, RESPECT ensures a fast start and lasting gains to motivate your present and ultimately enrich your future.

I spent my career at a world-class corporation as a global leader and learned the best executives use a streamlined set of principles for business and professional growth. Executives are taught to understand themselves, manage time, develop others, achieve goals, and embody core principles for success. Some core principles are stated repeatedly, such as: be proactive, set and share goals, and value others.

Be proactive, and you'll dodge problems. By thinking ahead and preparing a bit, you will save time, make a great impression, and get ahead of the rest.

Set and share bold but attainable goals and others will want to help and follow you. Goals don't need to be perfectly crafted to be effective. It's the process of achieveing those goals that gives a powerful feeling of accomplishment to all involved.

<u>Value others</u> to unlock ideas and hidden potential. Everyone has something unique to contribute and engaging sincerely with people delivers big returns.

If corporate progress can center on a few simple principles, personal progress can, too. RUN, REACH and RESPECT are those Principles.

> **RUN builds physical and mental well-being.**
>
> **REACH creates a life bigger than the present.**
>
> **RESPECT impacts the world.**

The Principles along with the Actions and Framework introduced here, will establish your strategy for daily, monthly, and lifelong personal progress. RUN, REACH, RESPECT is applicable to kids, teenagers, and adults. Whether you are striving for change, chronically overwhelmed, or already feeling fulfilled, RUN, REACH, RESPECT will enrich your life and the lives of those closest to you.

What makes RUN, REACH, RESPECT different? The Principles provide an uncomplicated approach to **overcoming inertia**. Inertia is the constraint that keeps businesses and people doing the same things in the same ways; it keeps us from growing and changing. On the positive side, inertia can be overcome with even the smallest outside force. RUN, REACH, RESPECT is the external force that gets you started and keeps you going.

When you're at work or in school, personal progress is often motivated by specific measures. You can earn more money, make good grades, work more hours, find a fulfilling job, or graduate to a new level. These built-in measures help you strive to achieve greater outcomes. Measures in your personal life are not as straightforward. RUN, REACH, RESPECT prompts you to define and measure the not-so-obvious improvements in all aspects of your life.

When I retired in my early 50s from a long corporate career, specific events made me realize the previous 15 to 20 years were a blur. Friends and family members reminded me of happy times, heartbreaks, and personal priorities I had ignored. These ruminations were the origin of RUN, REACH, RESPECT. My professional progress had overpowered my personal progress. I was fearful of repeating more years of blur, so I began defining what personal progress would mean to me.

I started by compiling a list of activities that are proven to impact overall well-being, such as exercising daily, eating less red meat, continuing education, taking up a hobby, and making new friends. My list grew and I noticed that many activities were redundant or not applicable to my age, abilities or interests. I wanted a short checklist of actions that would make the biggest impact on my life and the lives of those closest to me.

Build a Framework for personal progress.

Checklists have been used for centuries. The right ones have been proven to be freeing because they unlock personal capacity and create an organized approach to repeatable success. The use of well-researched checklists has significantly improved the quality and safety of air travel, construction, and medicine. Even the most experienced professionals need checklists. When we are under pressure or without a plan, it's hard to remember everything that should be done.[1]

When I applied my research on checklists to my long list, I found that most activities could be linked to three principles: Run, Reach, and Respect. RUN activities build physical and mental well-being. Efforts that cause you to REACH help create a life bigger than the present. Deeds of RESPECT impact the world.

RUN, REACH and RESPECT could have been **the** checklist I was looking for, but it's a bit short and vague.[2] With more research, I pinpointed 12 of the most well-established Actions for personal progress. I began using and sharing **this** list of high-impact Actions with excellent results:

PRINCIPLES

	RUN	REACH	RESPECT
ACTIONS	Get Active	Practice Your Intention	Be Kind
	Hydrate	Manage Your Money	Express Thanks
	Eat Nutrient-Rich	Expand Your Circle	Improve Your Environment
	Restore	Read	Reflect

Early feedback confirmed that the Actions apply to children, teenagers, and adults filling any role in life – professionals, parents, students, new or long-time employees, and retirees. Having established these Actions as essential for personal progress, I created the Framework I needed to keep myself accountable. Take a look at the Framework Except on the next page.

Applying the Framework made tracking, reviewing, and adjusting my Actions easy and repeatable. I was surprised when I felt more fulfilled after checking only 4 of the 12 Actions each day. When I completed 7 or more Actions a day, I felt really accomplished. Some who used the Framework said it was an effective way to focus on one Action they were struggling with, such as Eat Nutrient-Rich. Once the Action became ingrained, they moved on to another Action. Not only did the Framework help them measure personal progress, it motivated them to improve.

FRAMEWORK EXCERPT

January	1	2	3	4	5	6	7	8	28	29	30	31	#
RUN													
Get Active													
Hydrate													
Eat Nutrient-Rich													
Restore													
REACH													
Practice Your Intention													
Manage Your Money													
Expand Your Circle													
Read													
RESPECT													
Be Kind													
Express Thanks													
Improve Your Environment													
Reflect													

You will learn more about the studies that form the basis of RUN, REACH, RESPECT in later chapters and how the rationale, sets of Actions, and Framework replicate corporate strategies for success. Now I will share the approach that gets you started and keeps you going in the direction that matters most.

Track, Review, and Adjust.

Business management gurus agree that the best way to make big improvements is to track, review, and adjust. The Framework checklists at the back of this guide are ready for this purpose. You will check boxes to track your Actions. Then you'll tally the check marks in the # column at the end of each month to review where you've been focusing and not focusing your attention. Adjust when you see your Actions are not well distributed or are falling short. Use the Monthly Focus column to declare how you want to improve.

Unlike the use of critical industry checklists, there is no expectation to check all the boxes every day to achieve personal success. After a month, my use of the Framework confirmed steady personal progress. It also revealed that I needed to make changes to check-the-box on "difficult" Actions more consistently.

Which RUN, REACH, RESPECT Actions are natural for you, and where do you struggle?

_____

_____

_____

Admittedly, I struggle with "Be Kind." I think it's important to keep in touch with family and be giving of my time. After reviewing my checked boxes, it was clear that I was not conveying kindness by my definition. For example, I wanted to spend more time with my mom, but she lived 300 miles away, and my focus was elsewhere. I adjusted by making "Spend more time with Mom" a Monthly Focus on my Framework. Soon, I began calling my mom a lot more often and making more monthly visits. After adjusting Be Kind, I quickly began feeling that my new contributions were enriching me and those closest to me.

Maybe it's your diet or way of managing money that needs attention. Record these in the Monthly Focus column in your Framework. Your Monthly Focus may change or stay the same from month to month. Use this practice as needed to bring attention to difficult Actions or those that slip.

March	1	2	3	29	30	31	#	Monthly Focus
RUN								
Get Active								
Hydrate								Example: Drink 5 glasses of water per day
Eat Nutrient-Rich								
Restore								
REACH								
Practice Your Intention								
Manage Your Money								Example: Add $$$ to emergency savings account
Expand Your Circle								
Read								
RESPECT								
Be Kind								
Express Thanks								Example: Spend more time with Mom
Improve Your Environment								
Reflect								

The following graphic illustrates how tracking your Actions and reviewing your Framework will bring strong results. The adjustments you make by declaring a Monthly Focus will amplify your personal progress.

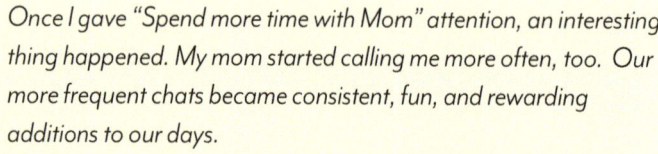

Once I gave "Spend more time with Mom" attention, an interesting thing happened. My mom started calling me more often, too. Our more frequent chats became consistent, fun, and rewarding additions to our days.

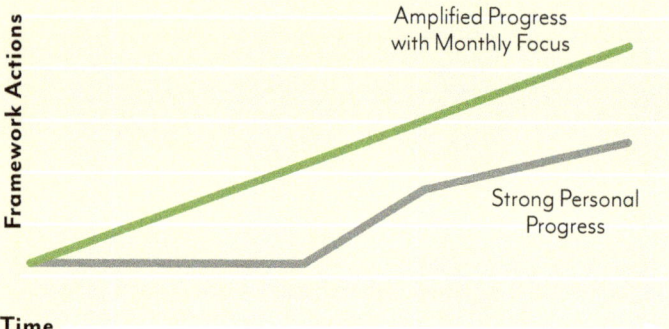

Use the Framework to track and review your Actions, adjust your Monthly Focus, and grow personal progress.

Remember, **there is no expectation to check 12 boxes every day**. Work on what is most important to you. Some people like to aim for checking the three, higher-level boxes of RUN, REACH and RESPECT and not the individual Actions. Others choose to focus on one Action per month. All are okay. Explore the Framework tracking options and practice what works best for you.

When you review your progress by tallying your checked boxes in the # column, don't worry if the monthly tallies vary wildly. They will. Just continue to make personal adjustments that motivate you and feel like progress.

Set an Intention to define your best self.

In a physical sense, checklists motivate us to overcome the inertia of life that keeps us from rising to our capabilities. The Framework is tangible and provides the built-in measures and tracking you need to make steady improvements. It can stand on its own and can be used as-is. But the mental force behind personal progress comes from setting your mission statement, your overarching goals, or your "Intention."

What do you want to accomplish most? What will bring you the greatest fulfillment? What is the new tomorrow you want to create? An Intention should be clear, positive, and within your control.[3]

Corporations define their **mission statements** to communicate purpose and direction and ensure sustainable success. The best mission statements concisely capture the company's culture and values. This corporate "intention" serves to help focus and motivate daily work, achieve goals, and innovate new products and services.

Mission statements are not only for corporations. Many successful people attribute their achievements to the mission statement or intention they live by.[4]

Drafting your Intention takes time. Explore your values and your short- and long-term goals. Consider what drives you and what brings you joy and peace. Once you settle on an Intention, it will capture your strengths, goals, and what makes you happy. It will be your mental guide.

You don't need to link your Intention to all of the Principles or Actions in this guide. The purpose of your Intention is to hone your motivations for a specific outcome, achievement, or way of life. You will review your Intention regularly and adjust it when needed.

> **Defining your Intention will ensure you "Start each day with promise."**

Use the Example Intentions below or from other resources, then begin writing and editing. Make your Intention time-bound or open-ended. Feel free to list multiple Intentions if condensing to one statement is too limiting. This is just a start. We'll come back to your Intention in the chapter on REACH.

EXAMPLE INTENTIONS
Excel at my (work, education, relationships) to create a better life for my family and myself.
Move to a new home, in a neighborhood I love, within three years.
Embrace joy and find ways to experience it more often.
Enhance my wealth by learning how to save and invest.
Complete (goal) by (date). (For example, I will travel to a new destination each year.)
Prosper and become recognized in my (sport, art, field of study).
Share more of myself to grow a loving circle of family and friends.
Have a loving partner and nurture the relationship.
Be independent. Find and grow a career that fulfills me.
Grow my spiritual practice and move forward through challenges and fears.
Enhance my health and fitness for more energy and well-being.
Support a cause that will benefit from my unique gifts.
Excel at what I do and inspire others to succeed.

Begin to draft your Intention(s).

RUN

RUN builds physical and mental well-being.

Although there is no significance to the order of the RUN, REACH, and RESPECT Principles, starting with RUN is the most straightforward. We all know the importance of exercise, a healthy diet, and rest. The Actions of RUN are the easiest to track, too. Defining the straightforward measures of RUN will benefit the more abstract measures of REACH and RESPECT discussed later.

> **The Framework makes the Actions of personal progress measurable.**

I'm not an athlete. I need to make a conscious effort to work out because I don't have a go-to sport. I prefer water to sodas, but drinking the recommended amount of water is an effort. The same holds true for healthy meals and relaxation. I generally have a healthy lifestyle, but I need to ensure I continue to eat well and reduce stress. The RUN Principle propels me to **Get Active, Hydrate, Eat Nutrient-Rich,** *and* **Restore.** *These four critical Actions boost my overall energy and well-being.*

All RUN, REACH, RESPECT Actions have been selected for their well-documented importance and unique attributes. Together they build the holistic Framework for personal progress. In each chapter, Examples of the Actions are provided as prompts. A Top Tip is also provided to help you choose activities and define measures that make checking-the-box clear and easy. It's up to you to match the intent of the Action to your interests and abilities. You decide what checks-the-box on your Framework.

Focus on your improvements and take credit for activities that are already a part of your lifestyle. It's encouraging to check-the-box on an Action that you know is a regular part of your day. If you already drink plenty of water, check-the-box. There's no need to do more unless you want to make more progress on that Action.

In the workplace, initial successes and those that repeat over time are known to improve personal performance through **psychological momentum**.[5] In other words, success breeds success. In the same way, the RUN, REACH, RESPECT Framework prompts and affirms your accomplishments to sustain your long-term personal progress.

Which RUN Action are you looking forward to improving?

_____

_____

_____

Get Active

The benefits of exercise on physical and mental well-being are proven. Studies show that "...aerobic exercise prepares your brain to learn, improves mood and attention, lowers stress and anxiety, helps stave off addiction, controls the sometimes-tumultuous effects of hormonal changes, and guards against and even reverses some of the effects of aging on the brain."[6]

> **Building the body is a mere side-effect.**

We're told the optimal baseline of moderate to strenuous physical activity is about 30 minutes/day, 5 times/week. Despite knowing this, many of us let workouts slip. We do not stay consistent. Get Active should get you out the door for a hike, online for a virtual class, or on the floor for push-ups. You will feel, look, and perform better when you Get Active. After using the Framework for a while, recognize how being flexible with your activities will keep you checking-the-box.

Flexibility is a key factor in forming lasting changes and staying on track. Don't feel like you need to work out at the same time or for the same amount of time every day. It's great if you do, but this is not a requirement for lasting success. If you allow flexibility in your Actions, you are more likely to make consistent progress, especially when your days are unpredictable.[7]

EXAMPLES

AEROBIC	WEIGHT BEARING
Run	Lift Weights
Walk/Hike/Bike	Play a Racquet Sport
Take a Fitness Class	Plank/Push-up/Squat
Swim/Surf/Snorkel	Golf
Row/Kayak	Jump Rope
Ski/Snow Board	Rock Climb

FLEXIBILITY	EVERYDAY LIFE
Stretch	Play a Sport
Practice Yoga	Do Yardwork/Garden
Practice Tai Chi	Do a Physically Intense Job
Dance	Clean/Do Housework
Use a Stability Ball	Take the Stairs

There are endless ways to Get Active. Examples are provided above to point out the range of options. Which of the Examples do you enjoy? Which ones are you already doing? As you personalize and define the daily activities that will check-the-box in your Framework, make flexibility your friend, but ensure you can measure the activities you choose. Define your activity in terms of something you can count; for instance, time, reps, rounds or distance, to simplify your tracking. Review your accomplishments by measuring frequency or increased ability and adjust as needed.

If flexibility is proven to be helpful when distractions of the day get in the way of your progress, then the Top Tip gives you even more liberty. You should determine your optimal weekly baseline of moderate to strenuous physical activity subject to your doctor's approval. But to Get Active consistently, declare a minimum, daily, go-to physical activity.

> **TOP TIP**
>
> Declare your daily, minimum, go-to activity.

My Get Active go-to activity is a set of push-ups. They keep my back and arms strong, engage my core, and they can be done anywhere. I've chosen a set of 25 bent-knee push-ups as my daily, minimum go-to. If I can complete 25 of these, my fitness level would be considered "excellent" for my age group.[8] A set of 25 push-ups is challenging, so when I complete them, I allow myself to check-the-box on Get Active for the day. This go-to activity makes me more active and more consistent.

If your go-to physical activity is to do housework, create a measure that is meaningful to you. It could be related to the number of rooms you clean or the time or effort you spent. If you have a physically demanding job, take credit for your time on those activities as your daily minimum. Others may not feel accomplished until they've run a 5K. As you move forward, define your activities for each Action based on your personal goals, abilities, time, and what progress means to you.

The Get Active Top Tip may sound like a cop-out, and it would be if you never did anything more than your daily minimum activity. If your doctor approves, every week should bring a variety of Get Active opportunities that equal about 150 minutes of moderate to strenuous activity. Recognize them, plan them, take them on, and check-the-box on your Framework.

How will you apply the Get Active Top Tip?

_____

_____

_____

_____

_____

_____

Hydrate

Hydrate is the least complicated Action on the checklist but it's still hard to meet the experts' recommendations. We are incredibly fortunate to have clean water available nearly everywhere in the United States. Yet, it is reported that most Americans are chronically dehydrated. Adverse effects are dry or bad skin, hunger, afternoon fatigue, slow memory, poor concentration, and irritability. It makes sense. About 60% of the human body is water. Consider these statistics: the brain, kidneys, heart, and lungs contain over 70% water, and the skin is 60-70% water. Our vital organs require this essential compound to operate, flush toxins, and stay healthy.[9] Water is said to be the body's delivery system for oxygen and nutrition, so dehydration can slow down mental capacity, energy, and digestion. Hydrate is critical for physical and mental well-being.

There are several rules of thumb for calculating the ideal daily hydration. Here is one:

0.70 x (body weight in pounds) = ounces of daily hydration

We require about 16 ounces of liquid, 4 to 9 times daily, depending on our weight. Not all of this liquid intake needs to be water, but it should be low in caffeine, sugar, and alcohol for effective hydration. Use the Examples for variety.

If you regularly eat fruits, vegetables, and brothy foods, you probably get 20% of your daily hydration from meals and can reduce your daily water intake proportionately.

Do a few calculations to determine what makes sense for you.

EXAMPLES [10]

Filtered Water	Enjoy your water still or sparkling, cold or warm.
Milk or Milk Alternatives	Get calcium, protein, and vitamin D.
Infused Water	Add fresh fruits, herbs, or vegetables for a refreshing flavor.
100% Juice	Choose low sugar and low/no sodium.
Tea	Boost immunity with antioxidants.
Sports Drinks	Make hydration quick and effective with electrolytes.
Coconut Water	Choose no/low sugar and no additives.
High Water-Content Foods	Eat watermelon, tomatoes, spinach, strawberries, pineapples, cucumbers, grapefruit, and lettuce, to name a few.

As soon as I get settled in bed, at my desk, or when I leave the house, I suddenly find myself thirsty. I purchased several 16-ounce reusable bottles, so I don't miss an opportunity to Hydrate. The bottles vary between glass, insulated, easy to carry, and easy to infuse. This variety encourages me to vary my hydrating drinks. Equal-size bottles simplify the measuring; I don't have to count the exact number of ounces. When I drink four to five bottles during the day, I check-the-box. I still drink coffee and don't meet the Hydrate suggestions as frequently as I should, but the measuring helps me to Hydrate better than I have in the past.

TOP TIP

Fill your water bottle; carry it, drink it, and refill it.

At a restaurant, assume a glass holds 16 to 20 ounces of water, and if you're buying hydrating drinks on-the-go, check the volume. After a while, gauging and counting will become second nature.

Counting bottles or ounces is not the only way to check-the-box. Decide what is progress for you. Will it be a steady increase in water compared to what you normally drink? Will it be one replacement daily of a sugary or alcoholic drink with a choice from the Examples? The equation for ideal hydration is "ideal." Check-the-box when you make progress toward your personal measure for improvement.

As you get started or change your hydration levels, don't overdo it. Some of the symptoms of overhydration mimic dehydration, such as headaches, nausea, and fatigue. When you have too much water in your body, the kidneys can't remove the excess, and the sodium in your blood becomes diluted. This can cause seizures, coma, or death.[11] Take it slow, and don't make significant or sudden changes in your liquid consumption.

What is the #1 change you will make to Hydrate?

_____

_____

_____

_____

_____

Eat Nutrient-Rich

Nutritionally dense foods are sometimes referred to as "superfoods." The attributes of eating a diet high in superfoods are similar to other diets that focus on general, long-term health, such as the Mediterranean Diet, Anti-Inflammatory Diet, or MIND Diet.

As the name suggests, a Mediterranean Diet follows the dietary habits of people who live near the Mediterranean Sea. Mediterranean diets are thought to improve longevity and physical and mental agility. Anti-inflammatory diets are recommended to minimize the debilitating effects of autoimmune diseases, such as rheumatoid arthritis. The MIND Diet suggests foods shown to improve brain health.

> **Diets that focus on long-term health share a short list of nutrient-rich foods or "superfoods."**

The benefits of healthy menu options and suggested recipes for dietary needs are highly published. Because many of the recommendations share the same nutrient-rich foods, creating grocery lists and selecting superfoods should be easy. But often, it's not the selection but the preparation that's difficult. Start by altering your grocery list to include ready-to-eat foods from the Examples, such as carrots, blueberries, nuts, and yogurt, and remove sugary or fatty snack foods that should not be on your grocery list.

Food Groups	EXAMPLES [12,13,14]	Common Superfoods
Dark leafy greens	Romaine, Swiss chard, collard greens, mustard greens, bok choy	Spinach, kale
Other vegetables	Squash, peppers, Brussels sprouts, cabbage, cauliflower, radishes, cucumbers	Broccoli, sweet potato, carrots
Berries	Grapes, strawberries, blackberries, cherries	Blueberries
Other fruits	Watermelon, papaya, mango, pomegranate, apples, banana, pears, dates	Avocado, citrus, tomatoes
Nuts and seeds	Almonds, peanuts, pistachios, hazelnuts, pecans	Walnuts
Legumes	Peas, black, kidney, red and garbanzo beans (hummus), fava, soybeans	Lentils
Fish & Shellfish	Tuna, mackerel, herring, trout, anchovies, sardines, shrimp, oysters, clams, crab, mussels	Salmon
Grains	Quinoa, flaxseed, wild and brown rice, bulgur, whole wheat bread and pasta	Oats
Protein	Eggs, turkey, poultry	Chicken
Dairy	Milk, cheese, kefir	Plain yogurt
Spices	Ginger, turmeric, onion, basil, mint, cinnamon, pepper, sage, nutmeg, rosemary	Garlic
Fats	Avocado oil, olives	Olive oil
Beverages	Wine, coffee	Water, green tea
Desserts	Dark chocolate	Fruit

In addition to carrying your water bottle, consider taking nutrient-rich foods with you when you're on the move. This will help you avoid the urge to grab empty-calorie snacks and meals that are everywhere. Highly processed fast foods and packaged snacks high in sugar, fat, and/or sodium are some of the unhealthiest foods. These have earned the name "junk foods." They satisfy short-term hunger or a dip in energy but undermine long-term health. Have nutrient-rich foods ready when you know you will be short on time or tempted by quick, empty calories.

TOP TIP

Make most of your snacks nutrient-rich.

After adding more nutrient-rich snacks to your diet, think of ways to combine other nutrient-rich foods for breakfast and lunch. Yogurt and fruit; whole-wheat toast and avocado; spinach, chickpeas, and pasta, are common suggestions. Now you have a new reason for choosing them. Add nutrient-rich snacks and meals incrementally and check-the-box on your progress.

> I had the good fortune of growing up in a Middle Eastern household. My Lebanese mother lived well into her 90s.[15] She always bought a variety of fruits, grew herbs and vegetables, and naturally prepared Mediterranean Diet meals every day. I try to replicate her cooking, but it doesn't happen often.
>
> When I grocery shop, I focus on buying ingredients with a longer shelf life for the meals I will eventually cook. Carrots, sweet potatoes, onions, garlic, romaine lettuce, whole wheat pasta, spinach, chicken stock, eggs, nuts, berries, and apples are on my grocery list. Canned beans, chicken, and frozen vegetables are always good for soups, salads, stews, and pasta dishes. I feel encouraged when I can put together a nutrient-rich meal or grab a good snack, even if I haven't been to the grocery store in a while. When foods I'm buying spoil before I prepare them, I make new choices.

Eat Nutrient-Rich to pack a variety of vitamins, protein, calcium, and fiber into your diet for body and brain-boosting benefits. I check-the-box when I eat 8 to 10 **different nutrient-rich foods** per day. Check-the-box on your Framework if you continue adhering to a good diet, make positive changes to your grocery list, or replace poor meal selections with superfoods.

What are your measures for Eat Nutrient-Rich?

_____

_____

_____

_____

Restore

Restore boosts your brain for better performance and stress reduction. Even if you don't "feel" stress, it's there. Restore is the perfect cap to the RUN checklist because it's critically important for overall well-being, productivity, and protection of your immune system.[16]

Start with sleep. Solid stretches of 7 to 9 hours of sleep are necessary to restore your body daily.[17] Some people have the good fortune of sleeping well; others need help to have a restful night. If you don't sleep well, please use your professional and online resources to work on restoring your sleep as the first step in your personal progress. Check-the-box when you are working on getting your best night's sleep. This could be setting a consistent bedtime, reducing electronics at night, or doing an evening wind-down activity to train your brain to relax.

Even when we get good nights of sleep, stress and fatigue can creep into our days. Recognizing anxiety-inducing events, avoiding taxing situations, or reducing them is easier said than done. For example, no matter our age or occupation, we often get carried away by stress-provoking social media. It often starts as a harmless means of exploration or procrastination but can spiral from there.

Restore can be a dream Action for your idle time because it increases your personal progress when you don't want to do anything else, and unlike social media, it doesn't have the potential anxiety-inducing effects. Nap, pray, or cook while avoiding other things, or use a free app to meditate while commuting or waiting for an appointment. Deliberately restoring yourself mid-day to maintain stamina and health can be done quickly. Use any of these Examples in place of social media to check-your-box.

> **Beware, social media can sabotage Restore.**

EXAMPLES

Sleep	Get 7 to 9 hours of sleep each day for the best health benefits.
Nap or Rest	Find a place to recharge for 20 to 40 minutes; nap, listen to music, or sit outdoors.
Meditate	Seek a guide in person or online. Mindfulness meditation will help you reduce anxiety, gain perspective on negativity, improve patience, and grow appreciation.
Worship	Cultivate spirituality with or without a religious or faith tradition to become more resilient.
Pray	Pray for a sense of peace and purpose.
Cook	Calm your mind in the kitchen. Improve the lives of others by sharing a meal.
Laugh	Be with your favorite people or seek comedic entertainment.
Play	Play with kids or pets. Participate in sports, cards, games, puzzles, music, or art.
Detox	Get a massage or other treatment to relax and/or cleanse your body.
Get Active	Run, walk, hike, dance, or practice yoga or tai chi. These activities relax the brain and build the body.

> **TOP TIP**
>
> Recognize what restores you, embrace it, and practice it.

As you apply RUN, REACH, and RESPECT Principles, notice that Restore Examples appear in other Actions. You'll find an intersection of Actions across the Framework. Use this to your advantage. The more you can link Actions, the more efficient you will become in achieving personal progress. Yes, take credit and check multiple boxes for a single activity while progressing in multiple areas. This is a Framework Bonus!

> *Yoga is a Framework Bonus for me. Yoga is my favorite way to Get Active and is truly a Restore activity for me. Check and check. I feel progress in both areas when I practice. This personal recognition was a breakthrough and caused me to focus on yoga more regularly on my path to personal progress.*

Recognizing and practicing what restores you will likely result in a Framework Bonus. Don't avoid Restore because you think it feels light or unnecessary. Use Restore as an easy Action to boost your well-being, productivity, immune system, and personal progress.

Which Restore activities will give you a Framework Bonus?

REACH

REACH creates a life bigger than the present.

REACH helps you create a personal and/or professional life bigger than the present. This is not to imply that your present life needs to be better, but instead, it is to ensure you guide your future with intention and fulfillment.

Companies often use **Return on Investment** (ROI) to calculate a project's potential success. ROI is an estimate of the benefit received relative to the total investment. This is an important concept because although REACH Actions can be time-intensive, they also have the highest potential return on our investment of time.

Time is our most precious resource, and it's the resource we all share equally. We can never replace wasted time; once lost, it's gone forever.[18] The Framework will motivate us to overcome the inertia of life that keeps us from making the most of our days. And once we are motivated, we should be thoughtful about where we want our investments of time to lead us. Since the difficulty we all face is making the most of our precious hours, the REACH Actions help us prioritize larger blocks of time wisely and deliberately.

> What do you want to accomplish most?
>
> What will bring you the greatest fulfillment?
>
> What do you want that you don't already have?
>
> What is the tomorrow you would like to create?

The REACH Action, **Practice Your Intention**, starts with a review of your Intention(s). If you are evaluating your lifestyle or experiencing a significant life event, consider it an invitation to look more closely at your Intention.

It may be the start of a new year. You may have accomplished your earlier goals, rejoiced in the birth of a family member, cleared a medical milestone, experienced profound grief, started a new job, or retired from a long career. Life events are gripping, and there is no shortage of advice to address the unique possibilities ahead.

Before writing, rewriting, or taking on a major change of your Intention(s), share it with others to sharpen your wording. When you Practice Your Intention, you will spend time shaping your best self.

Three more REACH Actions deserve your time.

- **Manage Your Money** prompts you to learn and apply fundamental activities to build wealth and remain financially independent into the future.

- **Expand Your Circle** urges you to grow relationships and experiences without forgetting to balance your time for long-term health and happiness.

- **Read** helps you achieve something deep — an understanding of feelings, cultures, unusual subjects, and even yourself. Read will expand your thinking for a life bigger than the present.

Which REACH Action(s) are you looking forward to improving?

_____

_____

_____

_____

Practice Your Intention

This Action moves your Intention off the page and into your life. If learning a foreign language, becoming proficient in a sport, or mastering a musical instrument is your Intention, you know it's important to carve out practice time each day. You will check-the-box when you allocate time toward building a new skill. But, if your Intention is more abstract, deciding what will check-the-box will take some thought.

You've already worked on a draft of your Intention. If you explored your values, and short-term and long-term goals, and considered what excites you and brings you peace, your Intention was probably difficult to write. Encapsulating values, goals, and happiness in your Intention takes a lot of reflection. Look at the Intention(s) you drafted earlier. Do more personal exploration if needed, then take your time to affirm, solidify, or redraft your Intention(s) here.

What is your Intention?

_____

_____

_____

_____

_____

_____

Now, begin to define your measures. Start by listing things you will do or are already doing to advance your Intention. Identify the significant activities, measures, or completion dates you want to achieve that are related to your Intention(s). Consider activities that are tangible measures of progress so that when you do them, checking-the-box in your Framework is clear-cut.

In business, adopting a **milestone schedule** lends accountability and a higher likelihood of success to a project. In personal life, if your Intention is to move to a new neighborhood, for example, list the steps needed to accomplish your Intention and add "milestones" or significant dates for the completion of each. If you are mastering a foreign language, set a practice schedule and list proficiency hurdles. Use the Intention Planner on page 74 to create your milestone schedule for success and check-the-boxes in your Framework when you complete the activities or measures you set for yourself.

**What measures will confirm you
are making progress on your Intention?**

_____
_____
_____
_____
_____
_____
_____
_____
_____
_____
_____
_____
_____
_____
_____

Broad EXAMPLES	Activities and Measures
Excel at work, school, or in family life	Write down your expectations; take deliberate actions to exceed expectations.
Move to a new neighborhood or city	Research the move, develop a plan, and complete steps related to the plan.
Embrace joy	List activities that bring you joy and experience them; review and repeat.
Enhance well-being	Practice RUN Actions, apply specific health, weight or laboratory diagnostic measures.
Enhance wealth	See Manage Your Money Examples, develop a plan; complete steps related to the plan.
Complete a goal, or Advance your education	Work backward from your desired completion date, define a timeline and the activities you will measure.
Master a skill	Record the number of hours per week you want/need to practice and proficiency levels you want to reach.
Make good decisions	Research decision-making processes and take credit when you apply them; (remember, we are all prone to making bad decisions).
Share my unique gifts	Actively contribute money, time, skills or other assets to help your favorite people or organizations.
Find a loving partner	Meet people who share your interests: take credit for joining clubs or activities you love.
Be independent, Be a model for success, or Grow confidence	Define what independence, success, or confidence means to you; check-the-box when you model those actions.

My father always instilled in my brother, sister, and me that we could do anything. My goals as a teenager were to get a good job and live in a nice city. These sounded like freedom and bliss to me. I don't know if my brother and sister took the advice to "do anything" as seriously as I did, but they lead successful lives today.

With encouragement from my dad, I completed a B.S. in engineering and an MBA in real estate, and by the time I reached 30, I had accomplished both "intentions" from years earlier. I was also happily married to my talented husband and pregnant with my first, adorable, baby girl. (My second wonderful daughter was born a few years later.) These were not expressed goals but, of course, happy additions.

In my 30s and 40s, I focused on 1) ensuring the well-being of my precious family, 2) advancing my career, and 3) retiring early. These were three (huge) expectations I had of myself. Effectively, they were my Intentions. It wasn't until after my retirement that I realized I had been overwhelmed with Intention for nearly two decades, and the time I spent on my Intentions was not as efficient as it could have been. As a result, I grossly neglected interpersonal priorities.

RUN, REACH, RESPECT helps direct Intentions and other personal priorities. To borrow the rationale for the Framework: When you're under pressure or without a plan, it's hard to remember everything that must be done. For two decades, I knew my Intentions, but I was not deliberate enough with my time and actions because I was under pressure and without a plan. Had I paused to recognize this, I would have had a more pleasant lifestyle and made a more positive impact on those closest to me.

> **TOP TIP**
>
> **Use the Framework to ensure this single Action doesn't become all-consuming.**

Through this reflection and rumination, at age 60, my Intention became: **Inspire personal progress in myself and others by creating a simple, adaptable guide.**

> *To follow my advice, I spent time refining my Intention to be sure it was clear, positive, and specific. I resigned from the miscellaneous roles I had taken post-retirement. These activities would not benefit my new Intention. And I wrote my measures:*
>
> | | |
> |---|---|
> | <u>January to May</u> | Read books and articles to find strong research and rationale for a guidebook. |
> | <u>February to May</u> | Write 600 words a day. |
> | <u>February</u> | Complete a summary. |
> | <u>March</u> | Get feedback from at least 25 people.[19] |
> | <u>April</u> | Determine help needed and hire great people to do what I can't do. |
> | <u>May</u> | Complete the first draft. |
> | <u>May to August</u> | Learn about, plan, and take steps to publish a book. |
> | <u>September to October</u> | Finish my 'personal progress guide'. |
> | <u>October to December</u> | Learn about distributing and selling. |
> | <u>January to March</u> | Promote RUN, REACH, RESPECT. |

When I started, it took me several weeks to get consistent, but I immediately felt good about my incremental progress. I came across many setbacks, too. Since I was a first-time writer, I was overly optimistic about my skills and schedule. I made many adjustments along the way. My milestone schedule slipped by over three months.

It is important to define and Practice Your Intention(s) because this will result in big accomplishments. In mid-life, without a plan, I got fewer returns on my increasing investments of time. My ROI was bad. This made me feel overwhelmed and exhausted. Had I created a Framework back then, it would have shown me I was sabotaging my personal progress. I was going overboard on REACH while neglecting RUN and RESPECT.

How will you balance RUN, REACH, and RESPECT?

_____

_____

_____

_____

_____

_____

Manage Your Money

Writing a few relevant pages on Manage Your Money is challenging because we all have different financial values and different levels of financial stability. Also, Manage Your Money is the most technically complex Action of RUN, REACH, RESPECT. There are colossal industries built around this subject. The information provided here is basic. As you identify your most important activities related to Manage Your Money, continue seeking financial education from trusted sources. Investment options, tax laws, and global economic factors constantly change. Don't get discouraged if you're unfamiliar with some subjects and new terminology. Ask questions and continue to learn as you apply this Action.

To be as concise as possible, Manage Your Money focuses on six priorities: Earn, Spend, Save, Invest, Share, and Thrive.[20] The chart on page 50 provides a definition for each priority and Examples of activities for achieving them. Before you continue, read the chart. This is a lot to take in, but remember you can always revert to the Top Tip for a fast start and early, positive results.

> My lifelong, closest friend is a successful entrepreneur and owner of cosmetology schools. Her schools have a robust curriculum and offer essential training to new hairdressers. One bit of sound financial advice is, "During the month, if you cannot pay a bill in full or make the minimum suggested payment, <u>at least pay some amount</u>."

TOP TIP

Review your finances, pay bills, and make consistent deposits two times per month.

Review your finances and pay a portion of a bill or mortgage twice a month, and you will:

- Be less likely to forget a payment.
- Keep your credit score high.
- Immediately save money on interest and fees.
- Check-the-box in your Framework – twice.
- Consistently improve your personal progress.

Consider savings, too. If you cannot match your savings or investment goal for the month, deposit what you can. Making a payment will keep you current in the eyes of a creditor and making a deposit will turn you into a consistent investor.

If you cannot meet important financial obligations or savings goals, ask for help. Many creditors and banks have assistance programs to help you get on track.

I identify as a first-generation American. My Syrian-American father grew up during the Great Depression in a small industrial city, and except for his time in WWII, he lived in the area all his life. It's where I grew up, too. My Lebanese mother lived in a village with olive groves and spring water until she was 29. She then immigrated to the United States, got married, and raised a family. She lived in and cared for our family home for more than 60 years.

My parents had extremely modest spending habits, and my father focused intensely on saving for his children's educations and the family's financial security. We talked about money a lot. Why we couldn't spend, why we needed to save, and what it meant to invest were regular conversations. I learned about the benefits of company-paid health insurance as a 10-year-old, not because we were ill, but because of its importance in financial security. This may sound intense, but I consider myself truly fortunate.

My husband and our daughters may not have considered themselves fortunate when I tried to convey the same money management practices. I inherited the need to underspend, save, and invest. There were many advantages to this outlook, but I know now that I could have taken more financial risks and enjoyed more indulgences along the way. I didn't consider spending that brings emotional rewards and enjoyment is also a key component of building wealth.

There's no denying that Manage Your Money is important for today's enjoyment and tomorrow's prosperity. Check-the-box in your Framework when progressing on short-term or long-term financial objectives. Every action you take to improve your earnings, reduce debt, save, and invest will allow you to spend, share, and thrive well into your future.

Until recently, I was managing my money but sometimes living uncomfortably. Some people spend too much without regard for future implications. As you Manage Your Money, be sure to pause and weigh the (present and future) opportunities you are giving up for the lifestyle you are living.

Which Manage your Money activities will you do first?

Priorities[21]	Definitions	Short-Term EXAMPLES (Do First)
Earn	Build a career that provides financial independence to match your lifestyle.	• Take deliberate actions during your workday to exceed expectations in an effort to steadily improve your income. • Understand your paystub, where taxes are going, and how much is remaining. • Be an entrepreneur and grow a side-business to expand earning opportunities.
Spend	Design a thoughtful budget and spend accordingly.	• Use a budgeting tool to list sources and uses of money; detail spending and expected income; find ways to reduce costs and increase income. • Always pay your bills (especially taxes) on time; if you can't pay in full, pay something, preferably twice a month. • Focus buying decisions on covering housing, food, health care, transportation, taxes, and education first.
Save	Build a savings account for needs or wants with a short time horizon.	• Keep an emergency savings account to cover 3-9 months of expenses. • If you have a specific savings goal, make regular contributions to an account separate from your emergency savings.
Invest	Take calculated risks to preserve and grow wealth for the long-term.	• Learn the "power of compounding" to understand how interest rates grow investments over time. • Calculate the estimated investment value you will need in retirement by dividing your desired annual income (excluding Social Security) by 0.04 (4%). • Open an investment account with a highly reputable company.
Share	Share resources consistent with your limits and interests.	• Donate things that are extra or not needed.
Thrive	Live well today and into the future.	• Understand "opportunity cost"; the choices you are making today have a future impact. • Establish an open dialog about money with your family. • Write a will, appoint an executor, ensure your beneficiaries are assigned to assets. • Protect yourself; don't succumb to phishing or get-rich-quick schemes. Apply all safeguards to reduce vulnerability to hackers.

Long-Term EXAMPLES (Do Over Time)

- Make automatic contributions to an IRA/Roth IRA and 401k; opt into employer plans.
- Continue your education and/or certifications to advance your career.
- Know the market value of your experience and strengths; go after what you're worth.

- Ensure you have appropriate insurance coverage.
- Budget for upgrades such as clothes, organic food, gym or club memberships, furniture, car, or a big vacation.
- Make automatic payments to pay off debt when possible.
- Update your budget.

- Reflect on your spending and savings habits; check against your values: Is what you are saving for worth what you are giving up?
- Encourage your children to save by matching the amount they save.

- Understand investment options and their calculated risks, for example, if you have a long time horizon before retirement, consider a portfolio that includes some aggressive investments such as stocks.
- Strategically diversify your investments with individual company stocks, mutual funds, and cash to balance risk, reward, and long-term goals.
- Make investment contributions beyond your IRA, Roth IRA, or 401k.

- Actively contribute time, money, skills, or other assets to help your favorite people or organizations.
- Understand the tax benefits of donating money and assets.

- Don't make assumptions on wealth or money management; get advice or data from experts.
- See an estate planner to decide on a revocable living trust, living will, healthcare power of attorney, or durable power of attorney for you and your family members.
- Maximize online safety by regularly changing passwords, using a different password for each site, turning on two-factor authentications, and encrypting your computer.

Expand Your Circle

There are excellent reasons to engage with friends and family, new people, and unique environments:

- Having warm relationships with people to talk to, visit, and count on improves happiness, mental health, and longevity.
- New settings and travel can keep you culturally aware and responsive to changing conditions.
- Interacting with people you trust is ideal for building a sense of safety, security, and confidence.
- Intentional or unintentional isolation can limit your personal and professional growth.

Conversely, spreading yourself too thin will blur your focus. Like most of the Actions, Expand Your Circle requires balance.

> *After I retired from a demanding career, I was keen to do everything my new freedom afforded me. I wanted to walk with friends, join a book club, become a member of multiple boards, start a company, teach university students, practice Arabic, practice yoga, bike ride, travel, visit family, and more. I quickly started expanding my circle into new areas. This was a good thing until it became too much of a good thing. Even though I was having fun, the activities distracted my personal progress. It took me five years to recognize that I needed to refocus my Intention.*

TOP TIP

Be committed to circles that support your personal progress. Practice saying "No" to others.

Your "circles" will help or hinder your Intention, personal enrichment, and fun. Look for the best people or organizations that can help you flourish. Accomplish this one-on-one, in a group, in person, or online. Remember that seeking the best people, places, and programs to connect with takes time. Choose your circles wisely and seek unbiased professional advice when needed. Expert advice is often the most undervalued or least considered means of expanding your circle. Your progress will be more easily achieved when others support you.

EXPAND SOCIALLY, PERSONALLY, AND PROFESSIONALLY

EXAMPLES
Stay in touch with family and friends to cultivate sincere relationships.
Connect your Intention to a community need and become involved.
Travel.
Start a business.
Start or join a book club or investment club.
Network with a professional group.
Join a sports league, social club, country club, or place of worship.
Share your knowledge; be a mentor; or join a board of directors or advisors.
Join a choir or musical group.
Seek out a mentor, coach, or counselor.

I know now I should have sought guidance before starting my "retired" life. Retirement is a life change. Life events don't happen often, and I should have sought professional resources to help me better articulate and manage what I wanted to achieve. In my case, I was overconfident and anxious to start my new life. After my commitments to new groups and activities multiplied, I pared down to focus on a short list of special interests. But I am careful not to narrow my circle too much. I need to stay socially, personally, and professionally connected to continue my personal progress.

> *I have a happy byproduct of throwing myself into varied situations in my retirement. My new, larger network of people and experiences are cultivating my refreshed Intention.*

We're all guilty of saying "Yes" to too many things. A corollary to Expand Your Circle is, "Know when to say no." This includes quitting groups and disconnecting with people hindering your personal growth. Respectfully decline opportunities and narrow your circles when you've expanded enough or too much.

With which people and experiences will you connect, and with which will you disconnect?

_____

_____

_____

_____

_____

_____

Read

Reading is most often associated with learning. Although learning is an important outcome, Read is included here because it is much more multi-dimensional. Read makes you smarter, keeps you current, offers relaxation and escape, and enhances your present and future. Read enables you to be a better student, helps you perform better at work, reduces boredom and depression, opens your eyes to new ways of thinking, and allows you to explore places you may never see otherwise.

We know Read is tied to academic success and higher prospects for children, but it can also influence job and income prospects for adults.[22] An engineer-turned-CEO once told me that reading the headlines (only) of the Wall Street Journal empowered him to feel up-to-date and confident in his profession. Read improves awareness for clearer thinking, better decision-making, and more engaging personal interactions.

> **Read is a natural Framework Bonus. Use Read as you Practice Your Intention, Manage Your Money or Expand Your Circle.**

You may prefer audiobooks, podcasts, lectures, blogs, and documentaries as your form of Read. These are enjoyable, practical, and time-efficient ways to check-the-box, too. You don't need to take Read literally, but just as social media doesn't Restore, it also doesn't check-the-box for Read.

EXAMPLES	
If Read is already an integral part of your life:	Use this Action to motivate you to explore new genres and subjects like poetry, finance, or high-tech advancements.
If you are a reluctant reader:	Get book recommendations. Start with easy page-turners or magazines to discover subjects you like. Try historical fiction, romance, memoirs, and books about animals, business, music, sports or travel.

TOP TIP

Read what enriches you.

Many of you are already great readers; I am not. The words often bounce around the page, and my comprehension is slow. I always enjoyed learning, but books were hard for me. I favored math problems and lectures, and since they made me feel accomplished, I avoided reading. That was until I joined a book club. At first, I thought it would be impossible to finish one book per month, but I surprised myself, and with practice, I got up to speed.

A book club[23] got me to read more books on diverse topics, heightened my ability to think creatively, improved my vocabulary, and gave me the confidence to write this guide. Now that I am a better reader, I've started exploring heavier subjects. And I know if it turns out that I don't like the book, I can say "no" and stop reading it.

If you don't have an amazing book club to keep you progressing, start one, or Read with kids or seniors to check-the-box on your Framework. Reading with others is one way to use RUN, REACH, RESPECT to enrich your life and the lives of those closest to you.

What will you Read?

_____
_____
_____
_____
_____
_____
_____
_____
_____
_____
_____
_____
_____
_____
_____

RESPECT

RESPECT impacts the world.

RESPECT is discussed last, but it's probably most important for a well-lived life. We depend on interactions with people and our environment for sustenance, safety, and esteem. Unpacking RESPECT into the four Actions of **Be Kind**, **Express Thanks**, **Improve Your Environment**, and **Reflect** may seem too simplistic to impact the world. But to strike a parallel from childhood, we are taught to live by one Golden Rule: Treat others as you would like to be treated.

Recognizing the importance of RESPECT, and putting it into action, can impact the world around you. Research on the **imitation effect** finds that people tend to imitate the actions of others as a means of social and interpersonal connection. Even actions that are dissimilar but are perceived to have the same result are often imitated for positive social outcomes.[24] This is true in business and personal settings. We can't control others or all aspects of our surroundings, but we can positively influence them through kindness, gratitude, environmental improvement, and reflection. RESPECT Actions can have a positive ripple effect on the world.

> **RESPECT is contagious.**

Unfortunately, negative behaviors are susceptible to the imitation effect, too. Envy, anger, and self-preservation are inborn. RESPECT Actions keep us from succumbing to the negative by expanding the positive. By integrating the four Actions into our lives, we will cancel negativity, attract what we value, and create a lifestyle of RESPECT. By doing so, we will nurture belonging, love, and inner fulfillment for ourselves and those we encounter.[25]

Which RESPECT Action are you looking forward to improving?

_____

_____

_____

_____

_____

Be Kind

When we express kindness toward others, our lives are equally enriched. Sometimes, we show kindness while expecting something in return. This is a natural form of kindness and is perfectly okay if the kindness is sincere. But science verifies that showing pure kindness —not expecting anything in return— benefits us physically and emotionally. Acts of pure kindness make us more connected and give us higher satisfaction with our lives.[26]

If you innately radiate kindness, give yourself full credit and check-the-box when your daily interactions with coworkers, friends, family, or strangers bring smiles of appreciation and gratitude. For the rest of us, we can start by being kind to those closest to us. After all, we should know what they need and value most. When we are kind to the people we are with most, we decrease tension, increase positive emotions, and demonstrate and share our best selves.

If you are dealing with self-inflicted negative or difficult emotions, encourage positive feelings by being kind to yourself first. We've all heard this advice, but self-kindness is hard. We tend to focus on what we have done or said that is wrong instead of the good outcomes we produced. The more you practice Be Kind, the warmer your internal and external relationships will be. Use the Examples to prompt kindness to others and practice being kind to yourself.

80% of Respect is kindness

EXAMPLES

Be Kind to Others

Nurture relationships. Engage sincerely and frequently with those closest to you. Call home!

Apologize if you were wrong or mean-spirited, or if your kindness was misguided.

Help a neighbor by taking out their trash, caring for their pets, or buying their groceries.

Personalize gifts and rewards. Know if the recipient would prefer cash, a present, or just quiet time.

Give a sincere compliment or praise.

Be inclusive and supportive of people who are left out, forgotten, or treated poorly. Help improve their situation.

Give people your attention. Listen, be on time, be patient, and be tolerant. Make eye contact and smile.

Send a handwritten note of appreciation.

Share your time. Play with kids. Be a mentor. Adopt a pet.

Cook a nutrient-rich meal and share it.

EXAMPLES cont.'d

Be Kind to Yourself

Practice the Third-Party Rule. Consider how an unrelated person would view the "situation" you caused. In most cases, you will realize what you said or did was trivial.

Take responsibility. If you made a big mistake, correct it or apologize - fast. This follow-up will ease your anxiety.

If you are feeling regret for things that cannot be undone, make a plan or take an action that will prevent a similar regret in the future.

If you are focusing on your mistakes, write them down along with your positive qualities and good results. Be generous and realistic. The positive will cancel the negative.

Stand up for yourself. Ask for help if needed to remove yourself from a harmful situation.

> **TOP TIP**
>
> Practice empathy, too.

We all know people who exhibit pure kindness in their daily lives. In my case, it was my brother-in-law, David. Every day he touched people's lives in ways that built trust and love, reduced stress, and promoted sincerity. David was not only a genuinely good listener, but he truly wanted the best for people. He acted quickly when he thought he could lighten a person's burden or help someone in need. Sadly, he died too early. The response we received at his funeral was both astounding and moving. After I experienced the outpouring of inspirational stories from friends, family, and his entire company, Be Kind became a priority for me. My brother-in-law's kindness, empathy, and actions improved the lives of hundreds of people. It's an admirable legacy.

People like my brother-in-law can understand the (stated or unstated) needs of others and can act in deep and meaningful ways. They intuitively know that kindness requires an understanding of the person and their circumstances. If a seemingly "kind" act was not appreciated, the giver did not understand the receiver's situation. Kindness requires empathy to best impact the world.

Some form of Be Kind shows up on my Monthly Focus regularly. I need to work on this. But I use and share the Be Kind to Yourself Examples a lot. Self-kindness helps me out of dark feelings and negative self-talk. I use the Examples that work for me to help others with their doubts and regrets. Offering Be Kind solutions to people can neutralize an issue, build confidence, and create positive emotions for both parties — a double act of kindness.

How will you Be Kind more often?

_____

_____

_____

_____

_____

Express Thanks

Express Thanks is a form of Be Kind, but it has a different purpose; it shares our appreciation for receiving something special. Expressing thanks helps us recognize the positive things in our lives. It lets people know we are grateful for the good things they are doing for us.

When we Express Thanks, we are acknowledging that something special is happening.

Some people start the day reciting or journaling an inventory of things they are grateful for. This is not a new concept. Structured religions, popular books, journals, and guided meditation propose methods for expressing thanks. Gratitude can be given to God, Allah, the Universe, our parents, teachers, or anyone we credit for improving our lives. Express Thanks is included here for its simplicity and benefits ranging from increased self-esteem to improved sleep. Even a better work-life can come from practicing gratitude.[27]

> *I created a gratitude list that is easy to recite yet inclusive of the multitude of important things in my life. One of the greatest gifts my mom gave me was teaching me the benefits of daily devotions. Here is mine:*
>
> *I am thankful for*
> - *my health and my home,*
> - *water and well-being,*
> - *my peace and prosperity,*
> - *safety and schools,*
> - *my family, friends, freedom, and food.*

I recite a gratitude list to relax and build positive feelings. The short refrain reminds me of everything I consider special and worthy of protection and appreciation. I use it to Express Thanks silently.

Check-the-box when you Express Thanks outwardly to others for the kindness they share and when you express gratitude inwardly for the good things in your life. This concept is so simple; I will spare the Examples and Top Tip.

What is your Top Tip for Express Thanks?

_____

_____

_____

_____

_____

Improve Your Environment

Be Kind and Express Thanks will create a ripple effect of RESPECT, and the same is true for Improve Your Environment. Notice this Action is not "improve the environment." World leaders and giant corporations are attempting to change the state of our global ecosystems. We should be conscious and concerned about the magnitude of the situation, but the focus here is on activities in our local area and personal spaces.

Improve Your Environment is about your home, community, workplace, and school. It's about bettering the environments you frequent to improve their feel.

We are beneficiaries and victims of our environments. We can't control where we were born or the people closest to us, but we can try to enhance the spaces around us to improve the situation for everyone involved. Disorder, clutter, dirt, litter, and confusion can cause stress, anxiety, and an overwhelming feeling of burden. Visual distractions can cause us to lose productivity and focus, whereas clean, orderly, and pleasant environments help us thrive.[28]

> **Most of the benefits of Improve Your Environment come from small, consistent activities.**

If environmental sustainability is your passion, this Action may seem light. But remember, RUN, REACH, RESPECT helps boost and give credit for your incremental personal progress. Over time, simple activities can make a broad impact on you and those around you.

EXAMPLES

Home	
Make your home as best as it can be with the resources you have.	• Declutter, donate, clean; organize your home, car, garage, or closet. • Garden, compost, do yard work. • Do laundry (in cold water). • Cook, limit carry out; reduce food and paper waste. • Unsubscribe from unwanted catalogs, email, and online and print subscriptions. • Reduce, reuse, and recycle, especially plastic and glass. • Keep your home safe, secure, maintained, and refreshed.
Community	
Take action to ensure your neighborhood is safe and clean.	• Pick up litter. • Shop locally; use reusable bags. • Walk or bike to run errands. • Apply safety and security practices.
Workplace	
Demonstrate leadership beyond your everyday responsibilities.	• Declutter; organize; simplify the workplace. • Clean up email; reduce email to others. • Bring your snacks, lunch, and water bottle. • Reduce paper and food waste. • Learn and share safety and security programs.
School	
Do things that are resume-worthy.	• Start an anti-litter campaign. • Encourage carpooling, public transportation, walking, and biking. • Pack a reusable water bottle to promote the imitation effect. • Be a leader.

> *Fortunately for me, cleaning is only one Example of Improve Your Environment. My daughters stay far away from me when I am cleaning the house. If I anticipate more than one hour of cleaning, I'm in a bad mood before I start. The funny thing is, I can't even watch others clean for an extended amount of time without feeling on edge.*
>
> *I do clean, but in small increments. I use a battery-powered hand vacuum to clean the dirt around the house. In 20 minutes, cat hair and dust balls are gone, and I feel great. The next day, I move on to another area for less than an hour of decluttering or refreshing. I check-the-box in my Framework when I make my environment look, feel, or function better.*

TOP TIP

Reduce, reuse, recycle, and refresh.

The Top Tip includes the well-known environmental activities reduce-reuse-recycle, but refresh is the important addition here. Refresh activities, such as decluttering, picking up litter, and maintaining the place, are contagious. As you begin making your environment visibly better, others will join in to make improvements, too. You will unleash the power of the imitation effect at home, in your neighborhood, at work, and at school to Improve Your Environment for the benefit of all.

In what ways are you motivated to Improve Your Environment?

_____

_____

_____

_____

_____

_____

Reflect

Reflect cements your personal progress. This guide has blank space for notetaking, tracking, journaling, planning, and reflecting. From an early age, we are taught to hand-write notes in school to better retain and apply new concepts. The physical act of using RUN, REACH, RESPECT as a working guide will cause you to Reflect and stimulate your brain in ways that typing, apps, or memorizing cannot.

> **Affirming your progress through reflection has a strong effect on self-motivation.**

In business, the **progress principle** explains that the more organizations and employees experience a sense of progress, the more likely they will continue to take action toward more progress. The same is true for us personally. We will perform better over time if we feel incremental progress and affirm achievements.

Note that the progress principle works only if your achievements are meaningful to you.[29] In every section of RUN, REACH, RESPECT, you are asked to consider what progress means to you. Take the time to Reflect as you work through the Actions. Forethought and meaningful adjustments to your activities will improve your results.

The act of writing has intrinsic benefits, but reflection can also come by way of quiet observation or sharing stories. The Reflect Examples provide a wide range of activities that check-the-box. Notice that meditation and prayer, often prescribed for self-help and personal growth, show up as Restore Examples, too – a Framework Bonus.

RESPECT

EXAMPLES	
Journal	Practice journaling to document actions and achievements, improve communication skills, and maintain a positive outlook.
Make a photo album, scrapbook, or cookbook	Document a life well-lived to develop deeper connections and share family culture.
Write stories, poetry, music; sketch or paint	Let your imagination take over for inspiration and improved decision-making and problem-solving.
Share family goals	Hold regular family meetings. Talk to those closest to you to share and support goals, problem solve, and help combat feelings of isolation.
Meditate	Learn mindfulness meditation to gain perspective, improve patience, and foster kindness and growth.
Pray	Pray as part of your religion or individual spirituality for a sense of peace and purpose.
Visualize	Visualize yourself succeeding; practice visualization to help you perform better for an important event and increase your confidence for a successful outcome.
Be proud	Acknowledge mistakes but focus on successes. You will gain far more by being proud, which will balance your perspective on failure.
Make a fresh start	Determine what is preventing or changing your rate of progress and start again.

TOP TIP

Use the Framework.

At one point, I could not stop reflecting on several bad decisions that affected my life and hurt others. This started a downward spiral. My ruminations caused me to write a list of bad decisions I made throughout my life, even at six years old! One negative led to another, and the list became two pages long. As I tried to escape this trap, I wondered what good came from these past mistakes.

So, I started writing down my good decisions. I used a side-by-side timeline dating back to my childhood. Soon, I felt a sense of accomplishment from the progress I saw on my second list. I let go of the regret and turned to what I could learn from both lists.

By focusing on the good, my regrets were largely replaced with gratitude. The two-column exercise also helped me unravel a few recent mistakes. This long reflection gave me a Framework Trifecta – Reflect, Be Kind (to myself) and Express Thanks (for a full life).

> **Don't reflect on setbacks. This can undermine your personal growth, maybe even more than progress can move you forward.**

RUN, REACH, RESPECT is designed to be self-fulfilling. Check-the-boxes, take notes, write affirmations, sketch, or document what you want to do next. Take full credit when you Reflect by using this guide. As you internalize RUN, REACH, RESPECT, you may think you can skip using the Framework or forgo taking notes because the Actions will become second nature. But remember, the best way to improve is to track, review, and adjust. Completing the Framework is a simple process that will ensure you check-the-box for Reflect and sustain personal progress.

How will you use Reflect to enhance your personal progress?

END EACH DAY WITH PROGRESS

Most self-improvement programs, personal development books, and even New Year's resolutions have a short life. RUN, REACH, RESPECT changes this by applying long-practiced business strategies to your personal progress. The Principles are the foundation for initiating your Actions and tracking, reviewing, and adjusting your outcomes for an organized approach to repeatable success.

RUN, REACH, RESPECT introduces a Framework of possibilities, not expectations. It's a structure for encouraging the Actions that define your progress. Remember, there is no expectation to check 12 boxes a day, 7 days a week. Use the Framework to transform your life alongside the demands of your day.

Share your accomplishments and learnings with family, friends, and coworkers. Also, share your Intention(s). This affirmation will be a positive reminder of your achievements underway. Many people want progress in their lives but struggle to define how to get there. Applying and sharing your simple path to continued optimism and success will enrich your life and the lives of those around you. You will start each day with promise and end each day with progress.

RUN, REACH, RESPECT powers your progress with approaches that motivate your present and ultimately enrich your future.

INTENTION PLANNER

January	1	2	3	4	5	6	7	8	9	10	11	12	13	14

February	1	2	3	4	5	6	7	8	9	10	11	12	13	14

March	1	2	3	4	5	6	7	8	9	10	11	12	13	14

April	1	2	3	4	5	6	7	8	9	10	11	12	13	14

May	1	2	3	4	5	6	7	8	9	10	11	12	13	14

June	1	2	3	4	5	6	7	8	9	10	11	12	13	14

END EACH DAY WITH PROGRESS

15	16	17	18	19	20	21	22	23	24	25	26	27	28	29	30	31

15	16	17	18	19	20	21	22	23	24	25	26	27	28	29

15	16	17	18	19	20	21	22	23	24	25	26	27	28	29	30	31

15	16	17	18	19	20	21	22	23	24	25	26	27	28	29	30

15	16	17	18	19	20	21	22	23	24	25	26	27	28	29	30	31

15	16	17	18	19	20	21	22	23	24	25	26	27	28	29	30

INTENTION PLANNER cont.'d

July	1	2	3	4	5	6	7	8	9	10	11	12	13	14

August	1	2	3	4	5	6	7	8	9	10	11	12	13	14

September	1	2	3	4	5	6	7	8	9	10	11	12	13	14

October	1	2	3	4	5	6	7	8	9	10	11	12	13	14

November	1	2	3	4	5	6	7	8	9	10	11	12	13	14

December	1	2	3	4	5	6	7	8	9	10	11	12	13	14

END EACH DAY WITH PROGRESS

15	16	17	18	19	20	21	22	23	24	25	26	27	28	29	30	31

15	16	17	18	19	20	21	22	23	24	25	26	27	28	29	30	31

15	16	17	18	19	20	21	22	23	24	25	26	27	28	29	30	

15	16	17	18	19	20	21	22	23	24	25	26	27	28	29	30	31

15	16	17	18	19	20	21	22	23	24	25	26	27	28	29	30	

15	16	17	18	19	20	21	22	23	24	25	26	27	28	29	30	31

FRAMEWORK

January	1	2	3	4	5	6	7	8	9	10	11	12	13	14	15	16
RUN																
Get Active																
Hydrate																
Eat Nutrient-Rich																
Restore																
REACH																
Practice Your Intention																
Manage Your Money																
Expand Your Circle																
Read																
RESPECT																
Be Kind																
Express Thanks																
Improve Your Environment																
Reflect																

17	18	19	20	21	22	23	24	25	26	27	28	29	30	31	#	**Monthly Focus**

END EACH DAY WITH PROGRESS

FRAMEWORK

February	1	2	3	4	5	6	7	8	9	10	11	12	13	14	15	16
RUN																
Get Active																
Hydrate																
Eat Nutrient-Rich																
Restore																
REACH																
Practice Your Intention																
Manage Your Money																
Expand Your Circle																
Read																
RESPECT																
Be Kind																
Express Thanks																
Improve Your Environment																
Reflect																

17	18	19	20	21	22	23	24	25	26	27	28	29		#	**Monthly Focus**

END EACH DAY WITH PROGRESS

FRAMEWORK

March	1	2	3	4	5	6	7	8	9	10	11	12	13	14	15	16
RUN																
Get Active																
Hydrate																
Eat Nutrient-Rich																
Restore																
REACH																
Practice Your Intention																
Manage Your Money																
Expand Your Circle																
Read																
RESPECT																
Be Kind																
Express Thanks																
Improve Your Environment																
Reflect																

_____

_____

_____

_____

_____

_____

_____

_____

17	18	19	20	21	22	23	24	25	26	27	28	29	30	31	#	Monthly Focus

FRAMEWORK

April	1	2	3	4	5	6	7	8	9	10	11	12	13	14	15	16
RUN																
Get Active																
Hydrate																
Eat Nutrient-Rich																
Restore																
REACH																
Practice Your Intention																
Manage Your Money																
Expand Your Circle																
Read																
RESPECT																
Be Kind																
Express Thanks																
Improve Your Environment																
Reflect																

_____

_____

_____

_____

_____

_____

_____

_____

_____

17	18	19	20	21	22	23	24	25	26	27	28	29	30	#	**Monthly Focus**

END EACH DAY WITH PROGRESS

FRAMEWORK

May	1	2	3	4	5	6	7	8	9	10	11	12	13	14	15	16
RUN																
Get Active																
Hydrate																
Eat Nutrient-Rich																
Restore																
REACH																
Practice Your Intention																
Manage Your Money																
Expand Your Circle																
Read																
RESPECT																
Be Kind																
Express Thanks																
Improve Your Environment																
Reflect																

_____

_____

_____

_____

_____

_____

_____

_____

_____

17	18	19	20	21	22	23	24	25	26	27	28	29	30	31	#	**Monthly Focus**

FRAMEWORK

June	1	2	3	4	5	6	7	8	9	10	11	12	13	14	15	16
RUN																
Get Active																
Hydrate																
Eat Nutrient-Rich																
Restore																
REACH																
Practice Your Intention																
Manage Your Money																
Expand Your Circle																
Read																
RESPECT																
Be Kind																
Express Thanks																
Improve Your Environment																
Reflect																

_____

_____

_____

_____

_____

_____

_____

_____

_____

17	18	19	20	21	22	23	24	25	26	27	28	29	30	#	**Monthly Focus**

END EACH DAY WITH PROGRESS

FRAMEWORK

July	1	2	3	4	5	6	7	8	9	10	11	12	13	14	15	16
RUN																
Get Active																
Hydrate																
Eat Nutrient-Rich																
Restore																
REACH																
Practice Your Intention																
Manage Your Money																
Expand Your Circle																
Read																
RESPECT																
Be Kind																
Express Thanks																
Improve Your Environment																
Reflect																

17	18	19	20	21	22	23	24	25	26	27	28	29	30	31	#	**Monthly Focus**

FRAMEWORK

August	1	2	3	4	5	6	7	8	9	10	11	12	13	14	15	16
RUN																
Get Active																
Hydrate																
Eat Nutrient-Rich																
Restore																
REACH																
Practice Your Intention																
Manage Your Money																
Expand Your Circle																
Read																
RESPECT																
Be Kind																
Express Thanks																
Improve Your Environment																
Reflect																

17	18	19	20	21	22	23	24	25	26	27	28	29	30	31	#	**Monthly Focus**

FRAMEWORK

September	1	2	3	4	5	6	7	8	9	10	11	12	13	14	15	16
RUN																
Get Active																
Hydrate																
Eat Nutrient-Rich																
Restore																
REACH																
Practice Your Intention																
Manage Your Money																
Expand Your Circle																
Read																
RESPECT																
Be Kind																
Express Thanks																
Improve Your Environment																
Reflect																

17	18	19	20	21	22	23	24	25	26	27	28	29	30	#	**Monthly Focus**

END EACH DAY WITH PROGRESS

FRAMEWORK

October	1	2	3	4	5	6	7	8	9	10	11	12	13	14	15	16
RUN																
Get Active																
Hydrate																
Eat Nutrient-Rich																
Restore																
REACH																
Practice Your Intention																
Manage Your Money																
Expand Your Circle																
Read																
RESPECT																
Be Kind																
Express Thanks																
Improve Your Environment																
Reflect																

_____

_____

_____

_____

_____

_____

_____

_____

_____

_____

17	18	19	20	21	22	23	24	25	26	27	28	29	30	31	#	Monthly Focus

FRAMEWORK

November	1	2	3	4	5	6	7	8	9	10	11	12	13	14	15	16
RUN																
Get Active																
Hydrate																
Eat Nutrient-Rich																
Restore																
REACH																
Practice Your Intention																
Manage Your Money																
Expand Your Circle																
Read																
RESPECT																
Be Kind																
Express Thanks																
Improve Your Environment																
Reflect																

_____

_____

_____

_____

_____

_____

_____

_____

17	18	19	20	21	22	23	24	25	26	27	28	29	30	#	**Monthly Focus**

FRAMEWORK

December	1	2	3	4	5	6	7	8	9	10	11	12	13	14	15	16
RUN																
Get Active																
Hydrate																
Eat Nutrient-Rich																
Restore																
REACH																
Practice Your Intention																
Manage Your Money																
Expand Your Circle																
Read																
RESPECT																
Be Kind																
Express Thanks																
Improve Your Environment																
Reflect																

17	18	19	20	21	22	23	24	25	26	27	28	29	30	31	#	**Monthly Focus**

References

The references provided in this section have influenced me and this guide. I'm grateful for the improvements they helped me make in my own life. Please contact me if comments, updates, or additions are warranted (runreachrespect@gmail.com).

[1] *The Checklist Manifesto, How to Get Things Right,* by Atul Gawande, 2010. Picador, New York, NY.

[2] If not a checklist, "Run, Reach, Respect" can become a great mantra - while walking - while meditating - when calming a stressful situation. A mantra can ground and lift by affirming our values or intentions and reducing self-judgment. See: *How to Deal with Stress in Your Life: Embrace It,* by Elizabeth Bernstein, WSJ, August 30, 2021.

[3] I first worked on this at the Human Performance Institute in Orlando, Florida. I was fortunate to attend the course led by its founder, Jim Loehr. See: *The Power of Full Engagement: Managing Energy, Not Time, Is the Key to High Performance and Personal Renewal,* by Jim Loehr and Tony Schwartz, 2003. Free Press, New York, NY.

[4] "Mission Statement," by David Gordon, updated June 27, 2022. https://www.investopedia.com/terms/m/missionstatement.asp.

[5] "Psychological Momentum—A Key to Continued Success," by Seppo E. Iso-Ahola and Charles O. Dotson, August 31, 2016. https://www.ncbi.nlm.nih.gov/pmc/articles/PMC5006010/

[6] *SPARK: The Revolutionary New Science of Exercise and the Brain,* by John J. Ratey, MD, 2008. Little, Brown and Company, New York, NY.

[7] *How to Change: The Science of Getting from Where You Are to Where You Want to Be,* by Katy Milkman, 2021. Portfolio/Penguin, New York, NY.

[8] https://www.topendsports.com/testing/tests/home-pushup.htm, accessed July 12, 2022.

9. "The Water in You: Water and the Human Body," by Water Science School, May 22, 2019. https://www.usgs.gov/special-topics/water-science-school/science/water-you-water-and-human-body.

10. "The Best (and Worst) Drinks to Keep you Hydrated," by Emma Kumer, updated July 11, 2022. https://www.tasteofhome.com/article/best-and-worst-hydrating-drinks-ranked/

11. "What Is Too Much Water Intake?" reviewed by Dan Brennan, MD, April 08, 2021. https://www.webmd.com/diet/what-is-too-much-water-intake.

12. "Mediterranean Diet 101: A Meal Plan and Beginners Guide," by Kris Gunnars, BSc and Rachael Link, MS, RD, Medically reviewed by Kim Chin, RD, October 25, 2021. https://www.healthline.com/nutrition/mediterranean-diet-meal-plan.

13. "Anti-Inflammatory Diet: What to Know," Medical News Today, by Jenna Fletcher, medically reviewed by Katherine Marengo LDN, RD, January 3, 2020. https://www.medicalnewstoday.com/articles/320233.

14. "Diet Review: MIND Diet, The Nutrition Source," Harvard T.H. Chan, School of Public Health, accessed August 6, 2022, https://www.hsph.harvard.edu/nutritionsource/healthy-weight/diet-reviews/mind-diet/.

15. God bless my mom, Elaine (Khoury) Jacobs. She was a beloved role model for all who knew her. Sadly, my mom died just before this book was finished. She lived a long, principled, and active life. I think she would have been proud that this simple guide models her advice for a life well lived.

16. "Can you eat and sleep your way to a stronger immune system?" by Madelyn Fernstrom, Ph.D., January 24, 2022. https://www.msnbc.com/know-your-value/can-you-eat-sleep-your-way-stronger-immune-system-n1287926.

[17] "How Much Sleep Do We Really Need?" by Eric Suni, updated April 13, 2022. https://www.sleepfoundation.org/how-sleep-works/how-much-sleep-do-we-really-need.

[18] *The Manager's Book of Lists*, by Sam Deep and Lyle Sussman, 1988. S.D.D. Publishers, Glenshaw, PA.

[19] Thank you, Linda August, Calvin August, Curtis Bailey, Katherine Berntzen, Rich Blazevich, Andy Bregger, Broad Braintrust, Janel Carroll, Winn Claybaugh, Alicia Dunams, Sam Deep, Jennifer Evans, Charlie Fusco, Vivian Gabriel, Sheila Hart, David Horn, Alexandra Horton, Charlotte Horton, Jacquelyn Horton, Jeff Horton, Ella Jacobs, Fred Jacobs, Shadi Mansour, Elaine Melonides, Amy Melzer, Dave Myers, Andrew Neyer, Kathleen Norris, Phil Rowland, Emmy Schroder, Lucy Schroder, Mamie Schroder, Mark Scott, Rob Snyder, Andy Walter, Mehwish Wasi, and Rita Cory Wittine.

[20] "Financial Education Handbook, Practical Ideas to Engage the Rising Generation," Bank of America Corporation, August 2020.

[21] Ibid.

[22] "Read a Book! It's Good for Your Career," by Bassam Kaado, Business News Daily, June 29, 2022. https://www.businessnewsdaily.com/9998-reading-helps-career.html.

[23] I encourage you to join or start a book club. I've gained so much from my impressive book club members: Jeralyn Barrett, Mindy Dankenbring, Sarah Fogarty, Donna Moloney King, Shirley Perry, Debbie Sanlorenzo, Mamie Schroder, Dee Stone, Ann Weigand, and Julie White.

[24] "Imitation of Action-Effects Increases Social Affiliation," by D. Dignath, G. Born, A. Eder, et al. Psychological Research, 2021. https://doi.org/10.1007/s00426-020-01378-1.

[25] *Be Nice (or Else!)* by Winn Claybaugh, 2011. Von Curtis Publishing, Laguna Beach, CA.

[26] "Why Being Kind Helps You, Too – Especially Now," by Elizabeth Bernstein, *Wall Street Journal*, August 12, 2020.

[27] "31 Benefits of Gratitude: The Ultimate Science-Backed Guide," by HH, August 1, 2020. https://www.happierhuman.com/benefits-of-gratitude/

[28] "5 Reasons Why a Clean Space Can Positively Impact Your Mental Health," by Joan M, September 5, 2020. https://www.cleanpacs.com/blogs/blog/a-clean-space-offers-health-benefits.

[29] "The Power of Small Wins," by Teresa B. Amabile and Steven J. Kramer, Harvard Business Review, May 2011. https://hbr.org/2011/05/the-power-of-small-wins.

www.ingramcontent.com/pod-product-compliance
Ingram Content Group UK Ltd.
Pitfield, Milton Keynes, MK11 3LW, UK
UKHW061223180426
11947UKWH00027B/1985